EVERYDAY LIFE IN

ROMAN TIMES

MIKE CORBISHLEY

SEA-TO-SEA

Mankato Collingwood London

This edition first published in 2006 by
Sea-to-Sea Publications
1980 Lookout Drive
North Mankato
Minnesota 56003

Printed in China

Library of Congress Cataloging-in-Publication Data:

Corbishley, Mike
  Everyday life in Roman times/Mike Corbishley
    p. cm. — (Clues to the past)
  Includes index.
  Originally published: New York: Franklin Watts, c1994
  ISBN 1-932889-79-5
  1. Rome—Civilization—Juvenile literature. 2. Rome—Social life and customs—Juvenile
literature. I. Title. II. Series.

DG272.C66 2005
937—dc22

2004063721

9 8 7 6 5 4 3 2

Published by arrangement with the Watts Publishing Group Ltd, London

Editor: Sarah Ridley
Designer: Alan Cassedy
Illustrators: Peter Kesteven and Ray Grinaway
Picture researcher: Joanne King

Photographs: Ancient Art and Architecture
Collection 7b, 18t, 20t, 25b; courtesy of the Trustees of the
British Museum 7t, 8t, 10t, 22t, 26t; Colchester Museums 24t;
Mike Corbishley 6t; Michael Holford 6c, 16t (both), 28t;
Museum of London 6b; Vindolanda Trust 14t; Roger White 12t;
reproduced by courtesy of the Yorkshire
Museum/Woodmansterne 5t, 30t.

CONTENTS

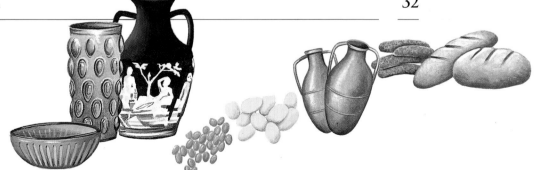

Two thousand years ago, the Romans were the most powerful nation in Europe and around the Mediterranean Sea. About 60 million people lived in the countries that made up their empire. The official language of all these people was Latin but they spoke their own languages as well – languages such as ancient Greek and Celtic.

Their empire began when the tribe known as the *Latins* took over the city of Rome in Italy and began to conquer the lands all around them. They became known as the Romans. Wherever they went they built towns and introduced Roman life, including the Latin language, to new peoples. You will find Latin words in several modern languages. Also, many towns in Europe were originally founded by the Romans.

Roman coins

This is a map (right) of what the Roman world looked like about 1,800 years ago. All these lands became part of the Roman Empire when they were conquered by the Roman army. Each new land (such as *Britannia* or *Arabia*) was known as a *province* of the Empire. Toward the end of the Roman period, this Empire was divided in two. The west was ruled from Rome and the east from Constantinople (now Istanbul in Turkey).

SOME IMPORTANT DATES FROM ROMAN TIMES

800-400 B.C.

753 Legend says Rome was founded by Romulus.

509 Latins throw Etruscans out of Rome. Roman state established.

400-100 B.C.

264-241, 221-183, 149-146 Rome at war with the Carthaginians.
218 Carthaginian general Hannibal crosses Alps with elephants to invade Italy.
146 Rome conquers North Africa and Greece.

100-0 B.C.

49 Julius Caesar becomes Roman dictator after several civil wars.
59-49 Caesar conquers Gaul and invades Britain.
27 Augustus becomes Rome's first emperor.

A.D. 0-100

14 Emperor Augustus dies.
c.30 Jesus Christ crucified.
43 Emperor Claudius conquers Britain.
79 Vesuvius erupts – Pompeii and Herculaneum destroyed.

WHAT DID THE ROMANS LOOK LIKE?

Some portraits of Roman people have survived. They show that you can't describe a typical Roman as the people looked different all around the Empire.

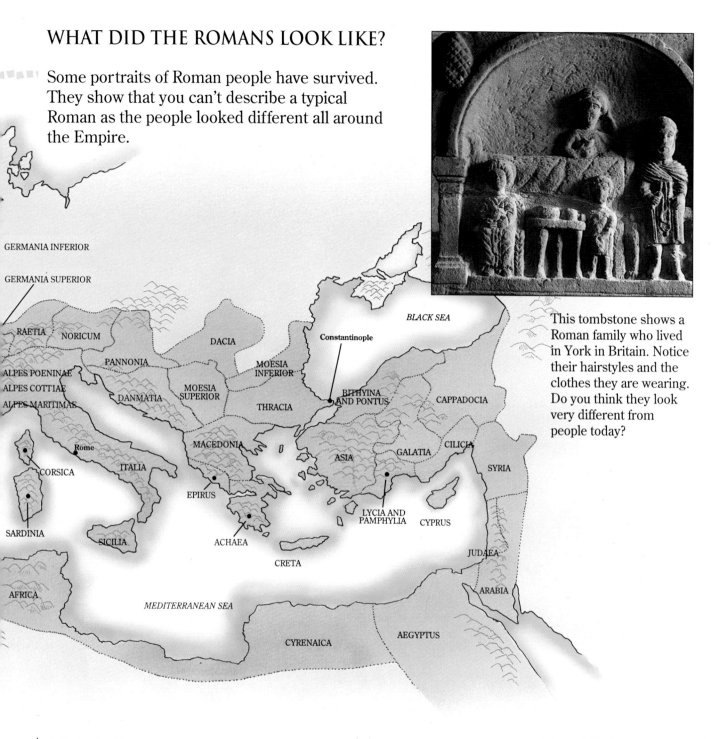

GERMANIA INFERIOR

GERMANIA SUPERIOR

RAETIA NORICUM

ALPES POENINAE

ALPES COTTIAE

ALPES MARITIMAE

DANMATIA

PANNONIA

DACIA

MOESIA SUPERIOR

MOESIA INFERIOR

BLACK SEA

Constantinople

THRACIA

BITHYINA AND PONTUS

CAPPADOCIA

Rome

ITALIA

MACEDONIA

CORSICA

EPIRUS

ASIA

GALATIA

CILICIA

SYRIA

SARDINIA

SICILIA

ACHAEA

LYCIA AND PAMPHYLIA

CYPRUS

CRETA

JUDAEA

AFRICA

MEDITERRANEAN SEA

ARABIA

CYRENAICA

AEGYPTUS

This tombstone shows a Roman family who lived in York in Britain. Notice their hairstyles and the clothes they are wearing. Do you think they look very different from people today?

A.D. 100-200

114 Emperor Trajan builds huge column in Rome to celebrate victories in war.
122 Hadrian's Wall begun in Britain.

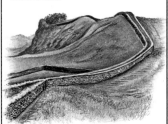

A.D. 200-300

212 All men (not women) in the *provinces* are made Roman citizens.
267 Athens captured by Goths.
284 Empire divided and ruled from two capitals.

A.D. 300-400

324 Constantine is Rome's first Christian emperor.
330 Emperor Constantine moves his capital and founds Constantinople.
367 Britain attacked by "barbarians."

A.D. 400-600

409 Vandal armies begin to invade Europe.
476 German armies throw out last emperor in Rome.
540 Roman armies from Constantinople reconquer Italy.

Detectives look for clues to help them solve crimes. Archaeologists and historians looking at the past call their clues evidence. We can find out about the Romans through three kinds of evidence – Roman writing, standing buildings, and the clues discovered by archaeologists.

Excavating a Roman site is a difficult business. Here archaeologists are carefully removing layers of earth, making a record of everything they find.

ARCHAEOLOGICAL EVIDENCE

What do you think happens to the things you throw away? When your trash can has been emptied, some things, such as paper and food remains, rot quite quickly. Other materials take longer to rot, like fabric and wood, and some will take years to rot, or won't rot at all, like metals and glass.

In the same way, only some objects from Roman times survive today. Many of these objects have been found in Roman trash pits (their waste dumps), Roman sites, or sometimes in Roman graves. Archaeologists have to decide what all this evidence means and what it tells them about life in Roman times. We often have more objects from rich people than poor people, for example.

Colorful mosaics on the floors of Roman houses give us all kinds of clues about everyday life. Here is the grape harvest being brought in for pressing into wine.

These Roman shoes have survived because the leather they are made from was preserved in wet ground.

ROMAN WRITING

The Romans left us a lot of their writing – histories of their empire, plays, poems, recipe books, and letters, for example. Very rarely do the original pieces of writing survive. However, we can still read today what the Romans wrote because many of their books were copied by hand by monks in the medieval period.

One letter that has survived was found at the site of Vindolanda, one of the forts of Hadrian's Wall, the Roman frontier in Britain. The letter was written in ink on a very thin piece of wood (see page 20 for more about writing). It is a party invitation asking Lepidinia to Claudia Severa's birthday party on September 3rd.

STANDING STRUCTURES

In some places, we don't have to search to find out what it was like in Roman times. Many Roman buildings have survived, especially in North Africa and in the eastern part of the Mediterranean. Sometimes the remains of whole towns survive, such as Pompeii which was buried under volcanic ash in A.D. 79.

This amphitheater, called the Colosseum, was built for gladiators to fight in as entertainment for the people of Rome (see pages 24-25). Much of the building has survived for two thousand years.

ON THE FARM

Have you ever seen anything like this before? It's a difficult question because one part is missing – the handle. It has rotted away but the rusty iron blade of this sickle has survived.

Farmworkers used sickles like this to cut crops in the fields. They grabbed a handful of oats or barley with one hand and cut through the tough stalks with the sickle.

The edge would have been kept very sharp with a sharpening stone called a whetstone.

FARMING

The Romans did not use machinery to farm as we usually do today. There were plows, of course, and a variety of special farm tools, but the most important "tool" a farmer had was the workforce. This was largely made up of slaves in the Roman world, people taken prisoner in the wars across the Empire.

Huge numbers of people had to be fed and bread was the staple food for many of them. The very poor people living in the capital city of Rome relied on free handouts of bread from the government. Most of the wheat needed for all that bread came from the Roman *province* of Egypt.

Not all farms in the Roman world were large estates worked by slave labor. There were many small farms, especially in Italy, worked by a family with only one or two slaves.

MYSTERY OBJECT

If you lived in Roman times you might have seen this clever piece of equipment on a farm. Can you guess what it is? You will find the answer on page 32.

Farm workers cut the barley with sickles in small fields near the *villa*.

SOME OF THE CROPS GROWN
BY THE ROMANS.

Radishes

Cabbages

Lettuces

Carrots

Oats

Barley

Dates

Apples

Pears

Cherries

Grapes

ON THE ROMAN VILLA

A big farming estate was called a *villa* – the word the Romans also used for a farmhouse or a country or beach house. Rich Romans often had a number of *villas* in different parts of a *province*, or in Italy itself. A farm might specialize in one crop or be "mixed," like the one pictured above.

When the owner wasn't on the farm, the work was supervised by a farm manager who usually had his own house. Nearby would have been a dormitory for the farm slaves as well as barns for animals, crops, and equipment.

IN THE KITCHEN

T his is a Roman food processor! It is for grinding up ingredients to make Roman meals. Today we call this useful piece of equipment a pestle (that's the grinder) and mortar (the bowl). The bowl has tiny pieces of grit set into the inside to make a rough grinding surface. Roman cooks used the pestle and mortar to grind up things like spices but it was also used to mix up sauces for cooking.

EATING OUT

Only wealthy Roman families had actual kitchens to prepare their meals. Everyone else either ate out, or cooked over a basic grill *brazier* in their home. This created a high fire risk in many Roman homes which were made of wood. So, various emperors made it illegal to cook at home, forcing people to eat out.

There were lots of different foods for sale for people walking through the town.

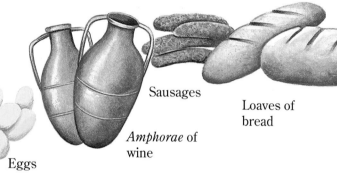

Sausages

Loaves of bread

Amphorae of wine

Eggs

Olives

Bars, like the one shown (*left*) from the Roman port of Ostia in Italy, sold a variety of snacks and drinks. Wall paintings showed the customers what was for sale – eggs, turnips, and green olives, for example. You might have a glass of honey water to drink or hot spiced wine. There were tables and benches inside or you could just eat and drink at the bar.

Slaves did the cooking in the Roman kitchen.
They would be kept busy preparing meals and
banquets for their master and mistress.

MAKE YOUR OWN
S W E E T S

You can make real Roman sweets at home.
Here are two recipes from a Roman
recipe writer called Apicius.

STUFFED DATES:

Take the pits out of the
dates. Now fill the insides
with nuts or pine kernels or
ground pepper. Roll the
dates in salt and fry them in
warmed honey.

HONEYED BREAD:

Remove the crusts from a
whole wheat loaf and break into
pieces (not too small). Soak the
pieces in milk and fry in olive oil.
Pour over some
honey before
serving.

IN THE KITCHEN

Romans ate their food highly spiced with
lots of different ingredients. Roman cooks
made their own sauces but they also
bought one called *liquamen* which was
made from salted fish and fish insides.

Cooking was done in ovens or over a
little fire on the surface. An iron grid held
the metal pans over the hot charcoal.
Vegetables and herbs were hung up to dry.
There were always some very large
pottery containers for storing flour, wine,
liquamen, or dried vegetables.

This is a couch from the Roman town of Herculaneum. Only the wooden frame survives now but originally it would have been upholstered; stuffing covered with colored material would have been used to make it soft. Cushions, stuffed with wool, feathers, or straw, would have made this a very comfortable piece of furniture.

TYPES OF HOUSES

If you could afford it you would live, with your family and slaves, in a private house with rooms set around an inner courtyard open to the sky. There would be more rooms at the back of the house around a garden.

But many people lived in blocks of apartments in towns and rented a single room or an apartment. In Rome these blocks of apartments were five or six stories high but elsewhere they were usually only two or three stories high.

IN THE GARDEN

Rich peoples' houses had gardens surrounded by a covered walk which shaded them from the sun. The garden was usually laid out very carefully with hedges of the box tree. You would see herbs and fruit trees there, as well as flowers. Many gardens had fountains and water basins. Statues were popular in gardens, too, and some statues even had their own fountains built in.

Grapevines

Fennel

Mint

Parsley

Bay tree

Fig tree

Apple tree

Cherry tree

The mistress of the house in one of the "living" rooms. Notice the low table and cupboard – like our furniture today.

Mosaic from a living room floor at Lullingstone Roman *villa*, England.

WALLS AND FLOORS

The Romans liked their houses to be decorated. They had not invented wallpaper but they did bring in artists to paint pictures on the walls. Owners of houses also hung painted wood panels on their walls. Sometimes the panels were plain but more often they showed a scene.

The favorite type of high quality flooring was the mosaic. This was made from little tiles of different colored stone or brick. Artists set the thousands of pieces into elaborate patterns or pictures.

Common mosaic patterns

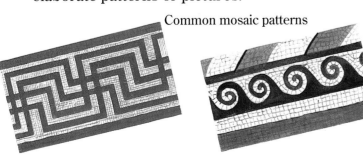

WHAT WILL I WEAR TODAY?

This is a leather sandal made for a Roman lady who lived in Britain. We even know the name of the shoemaker. He stamped his name on the sole. It reads L. AEB. THALES T.F. which is short for Lucius Aebutius Thales, son of Titus. This sandal was of the highest quality, perhaps to wear on special occasions when guests came to the house. You can see it's very like ones still used today. Do you have a pair of sandals like this?

CLOTHES FOR ALL

You can see from the drawings in this book what kinds of clothes Roman people wore. However, very few actual clothes survive as fabric and leather rots quickly. We know what the Romans wore mostly from statues and paintings.

Men, women, and children wore underclothes. The clothes people wore over these showed what type of people they were. Slaves and working people wore tunics, and in some colder parts of the Roman world they even wore trousers.

A Roman lady would wear an under tunic, and then a long dress. In cold weather, she would wear a very large shawl to cover her head and body when she went outside.

If a man was a Roman citizen then he could wear the *toga* over his tunic. Children wore simple tunics like those worn by their parents.

SOME ROMAN WORDS FOR CLOTHES

Bracae - skintight trousers worn under a tunic
Palla - shawl worn by women over head and shoulders
Petasus - hat with a broad brim to keep off the sun and the rain
Reticulum - hair net
Stola - woman's long dress

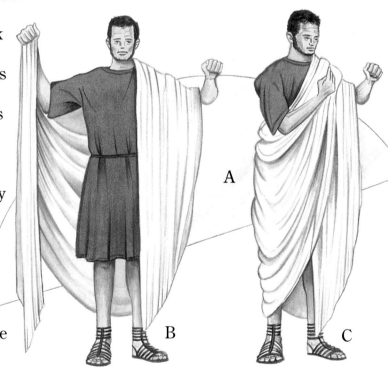

HOW TO TIE YOUR TOGA

The *toga* (A) was semicircular in shape. Its width was three times the height of the person wearing it. To put it on, the man had to drape one corner over the left shoulder until it reached his foot (B). He passed the other end under his right arm and across his left shoulder (C). It then had to be pinned with a brooch, tucked, and held in place.

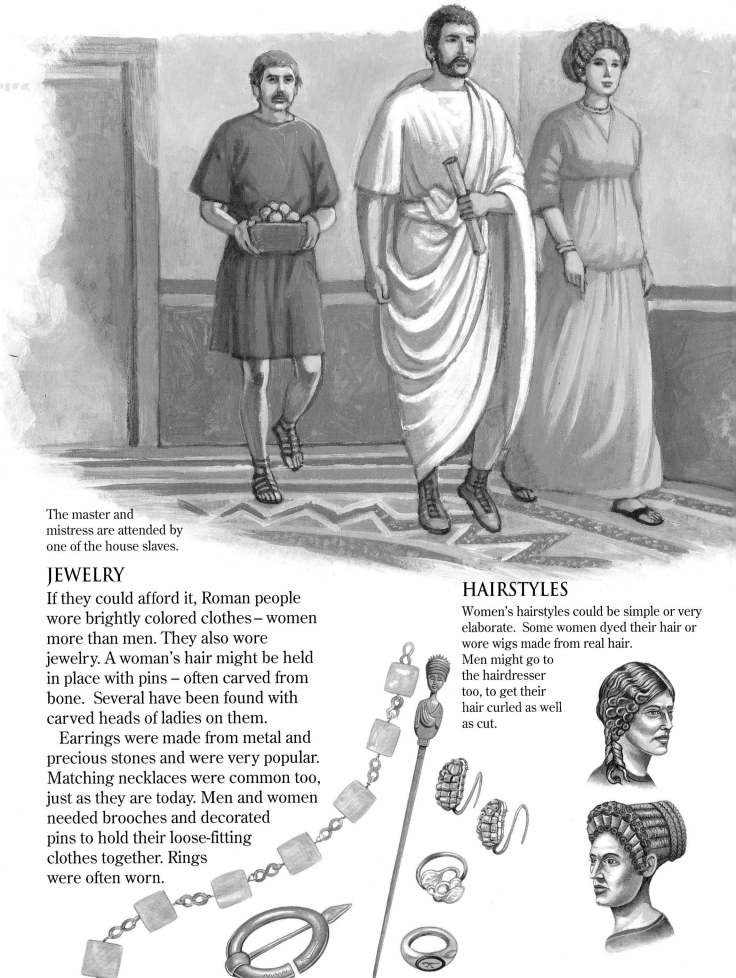

The master and mistress are attended by one of the house slaves.

JEWELRY

If they could afford it, Roman people wore brightly colored clothes – women more than men. They also wore jewelry. A woman's hair might be held in place with pins – often carved from bone. Several have been found with carved heads of ladies on them.

Earrings were made from metal and precious stones and were very popular. Matching necklaces were common too, just as they are today. Men and women needed brooches and decorated pins to hold their loose-fitting clothes together. Rings were often worn.

HAIRSTYLES

Women's hairstyles could be simple or very elaborate. Some women dyed their hair or wore wigs made from real hair.

Men might go to the hairdresser too, to get their hair curled as well as cut.

KEEPING CLEAN

Imagine life without soap! The Romans hadn't discovered soap so they found other ways of getting rid of the dirt. In the bathhouse, warm olive oil mixed with pumice stone powder was rubbed into the skin. The body would sweat in the heat and the steam. Sweat, dirt, and oil would then be scraped off with this instrument, called a *strigil*. It was usually slaves who performed this work.

Strigil

Oil flask

IN THE BATHHOUSE

All Roman towns had at least one public bathhouse. A bathhouse was cheap to enter and free for children. But it was not at all like having a bath today, or even going to a modern spa or health club.

First you undressed and went into a cold room for a cold dip. From there you went to a warm room and then into the really hot steamy room and a hot dip. Sometime later, after a slave had massaged oil into your skin and scraped it off with a *strigil,* you went back to the cold room for a cold dip. You might then even exercise a bit outside.

1. Dressing room
2. Hot steamy room with hot bath
3. Cold dip bath
4. Exercise yard
5. Open pool

MARJORIE MILLS PUBLIC SCHOOL

MAKING THE BATHS WORK

A large number of slaves were needed to make the baths work. The rooms were heated by a system known as a *hypocaust*. A furnace was lit and hot air was blasted under the raised floors and behind the walls of the rooms. The nearer to the furnace, the hotter the room. Water was heated in great caldrons over the furnace and then carried into the baths.

Men and women did not go to the bathhouse together – there were separate sessions. It was a place to go to relax, chat with friends, have a bite to eat, or even to conduct some business.

RELAXING

One of the favorite activities in the bathhouse was to play games and the Romans also liked to bet. There were games with knucklebones, which were thrown to see which side they landed on. Romans also played dice, either betting on what number would be thrown or using it to play a board game with colored counters.

MYSTERY
O B J E C T

This little object is made of bronze. It is only 2½ in (6 cm) long and could easily be carried on a belt or in a little bag. It would be of great use to anyone wanting to get really clean in the baths.
Can you guess what it was used for?
The answer is on page 32.

GOING SHOPPING

T his Roman tombstone tells us a lot about life at the time. Waiting for the butcher to prepare her order, this Roman housewife sits in a comfortable chair with her shopping list in front of her. Can you see what the butcher has hung up for sale? He is chopping meat, perhaps chops, on a three-legged block. Some butchers still use these today.

THE SHOPS

Shops in Roman towns were open onto the street. In the early morning, the shopkeeper opened up the padlocks which secured the shutters to the pavement. Some shops had signs advertizing their trade – a leg of pork for a butcher's, for example.

Most Roman shops actually produced their goods for sale on the premises. If you went to buy fresh bread, you would see the flour being ground, the dough made, and the bread being baked in a large oven.

The Romans used money to buy things, just as we do today. One emperor even fixed the price of all goods and services right across the huge Empire.

All coins had the emperor's head on one side. The coin with the smallest value was the *as,* followed by the *dupondius,* the *sestertius,* the *denarius,* and finally the *aureus.*

This was painted on the doorway of the shop of a clothmaker called Verecundus who lived in the city of Pompeii. Under the paintings of gods with elephants, the artist has shown wool being cleaned, woven, and then sold at the counter.

Roman streets were always very busy and noisy when the shops were open – in fact several writers complained about the noise and the dirt.

SOME OF THE GOODS AVAILABLE ON A ROMAN SHOPPING STREET

Comb and mirror

Pillow

Swan to eat

Fancy glassware and pottery

THINGS TO BUY

There were no supermarkets in Roman towns so shoppers had to go from one place to another to buy all they needed. Many shopkeepers and craftspeople lived in rooms behind, or on top of, their shops and workshops. Their work often spilled out onto the sidewalk, as it does in towns in many parts of the world today.

The countryside around the town provided fresh produce to sell in the shops, or more likely in the open-air markets in the town's squares. People also hawked goods in the street, selling items such as sausages and pease-puddings from trays carried on their head.

This object shows one of the ways the Romans used to write things down. It is a reusable writing tablet. The wooden frame held a wax surface. The writing was done with the other object shown, called a *stylus*. The sharp end was for scratching the letters onto the surface of the wax. The other flat end was used to rub the words out. When the wax became too thin to write on, more heated wax had to be poured into the wooden frame.

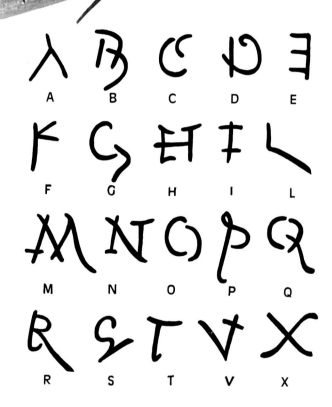

WRITING MATERIALS

Wax tablets were not the only things the Romans wrote on. Thin layers of wood were written on with pen and ink. Books were written on scrolls made of papyrus. Papyrus is a special water plant found mainly in Egypt. The best and most expensive surface the Romans used to write on is called vellum. This is the skin of an animal such as a goat or a lamb which has been made as thin as paper.

You can see Roman numerals in use today. Look for them on watches and clocks. You will also find them on inscriptions cut into stone on public buildings.

THE ROMAN ALPHABET IS SHOWN ABOVE.
TRY USING IT TO WRITE A SENTENCE LIKE THE ONE BELOW.

READ ALL ABOUT THE ROMANS

CAN YOU READ WHAT IT SAYS?

Few girls went to secondary school.
Roman fathers usually considered it a
waste to educate their daughters.

WRITERS

Homer wrote two long poems in Greek in about
800 B.C.; the *Iliad* and the *Odyssey*.
Virgil was born in 70 B.C. and wrote an epic poem
about the foundation of Rome, called the *Aeneid,* among
other poems.
Cicero was a Roman politician born in 106 B.C. He was
famous for his public speeches which were published
and used in schools.
Julius Caesar wrote accounts of his own military
campaigns against the Gauls which were used in
schools as history books.
Seneca wrote an enormous number of books during
his lifetime, mainly about the way Romans should
conduct their lives.

THE SCHOOL

Boys, and some girls, went to their first
school at the age of seven. They learned the
basic subjects of reading, writing, and
arithmetic from schoolmasters who set up
schools in rented rooms or in their own
houses. At age twelve, pupils went on to a
secondary school to be taught by a teacher
called a *grammaticus.* They studied the
literature of the Greeks (like Homer) and the
Romans (like Virgil), history, arithmetic,
geometry, and astronomy.

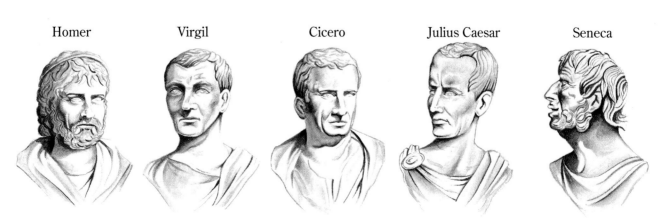

Homer   Virgil   Cicero   Julius Caesar   Seneca

MAKING JOURNEYS

The Romans did not have signposts but they did have milestones. This one comes from north Wales. Like other Roman milestones, it gives the number of miles to or from a place. Can you see KANOVIO M P V111? This means 8 (VIII) miles (M P) from a place called Kanovium. The letters and numbers on the stone would have stood out clearly because they would have been painted with bright colors.

THE NEED FOR ROADS

You can see from the map on pages 4–5 just how big the Roman Empire was. Many people needed to travel as fast as they could across it. The army had to reach trouble spots, merchants needed to carry goods, and officials needed to travel to govern the Empire. The Emperor Augustus developed an official courier service to carry both letters and people traveling on public business.

Roads had to be built everywhere. At first this was the army's job as they conquered new lands. After these lands became Roman property, it was up to the local government to maintain them and build new ones.

The Romans built their roads as straight as possible, to make travel speedy. The surface was raised above the surrounding land to keep it free from water. Layers of gravel and stone were pounded down to make a durable surface.

A horse-drawn stagecoach was the normal way to travel around the country. The stagecoach had wheels with iron rims and no springs so it was uncomfortable to travel in. A traveler could only expect to cover 5 mi (8 km) a day.

COVERING LONG DISTANCES

Traveling by road was a dirty business. In summer it was bumpy and dusty; in winter it was wet and muddy. There were stagecoaches for people to travel in – some people sat inside and some on top.

We know that most Romans disliked sea travel but for very long distances there was sometimes no choice. Ships were used mainly to carry goods and could travel up to 100 mi (160 km) in a day. Throughout the Roman Empire there were harbors and lighthouses.

Transporting wine   Carrying supplies   Cart for farm produce   Roman cargo ship

24 GOING TO A SHOW

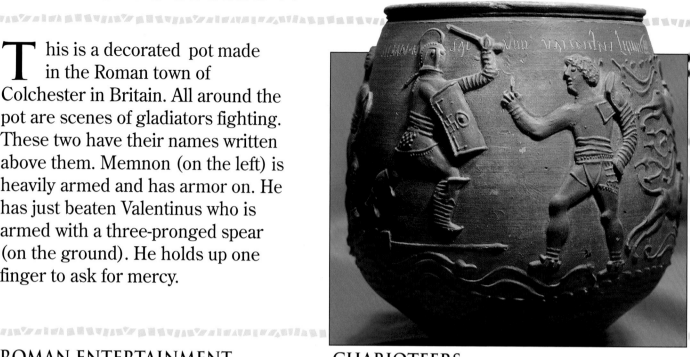

Thia is a decorated pot made in the Roman town of Colchester in Britain. All around the pot are scenes of gladiators fighting. These two have their names written above them. Memnon (on the left) is heavily armed and has armor on. He has just beaten Valentinus who is armed with a three-pronged spear (on the ground). He holds up one finger to ask for mercy.

ROMAN ENTERTAINMENT

Romans who lived in towns had a variety of shows to go to as well as the fights between gladiators. There were also theaters and chariot races. Special buildings were put up for these sports and entertainment. Thousands attended, perhaps 20,000 to a play at the theater, 50,000 to watch the gladiators, and 200,000 at the chariot races.

CHARIOTEERS

Charioteers drove chariots pulled by four horses and competed in four separate teams. They wore the team's colors – the Reds, the Blues, the Greens, and the Whites. The teams had to complete seven laps in all. Romans loved to bet on the races and charioteers could become millionaires.

Gladiators usually fought to the death. The crowd loved to watch these horrible fights but sometimes spared a loser's life.

Actors preparing for a performance.

MUSIC AND THEATER

There were plenty of opportunities for Romans to watch plays and listen to music in the theater. They liked Greek plays, both serious ones and comedies, but there were Roman playwrights, too. Actors wore face masks to help project their voices in the huge theaters. The type of mask and the costume worn helped the audience understand the story. For example, actors wore red wigs to play slaves and purple clothes to play young men. Music was usually performed as part of theater plays but concerts were given as well, often in a little theater called an *odeon*.

IN THE ARMY

Roman soldiers wore specially designed helmets. This one is made of iron with bronze decoration. Apart from the head protection, there would have been a neck guard and cheek pieces. This helmet was used by a soldier who fought on horseback, called a cavalryman. The helmets worn by footsoldiers, known as legionaries, were very similar.

FIGHTING WEAPONS

The helmet was only part of a soldier's equipment for battle. He also wore body armor, made of hinged metal plates or chain mail. His shield protected him, too. This consisted of thin strips of wood glued together. Felt or leather was glued onto the layered wood. The Roman soldier's main weapon was a short sword with a blade about 20 in (50 cm) long. He also carried a dagger and spears.

The shield weighed about 13 lb (6 kg) and was decorated with metal strips and paint.

A legionary soldier's body armor. Iron plates were hinged to fit the body tightly but allowed the soldier to move and fight.

The iron sword in its decorated scabbard was carried on the soldier's right side.

Daggers were often decorated and were about 10 in (25 cm) long.

Each legionary soldier carried two spears for battle. The long iron tip was fitted onto a wooden shaft.

Guards were posted along the walls, on the
guard towers and at the fort's four gates.

SOLDIERS OF RANK

As in any army, there were Roman soldiers
of different rank and soldiers for particular
jobs.

Legionary   Cavalryman   Standard
                                        bearer

Centurion   Auxiliary

THE FORT

Roman forts were always laid out very
carefully by the army's engineers. Each
night, when the army was on the march, a
temporary camp was made. The soldiers
slept under leather tents.

But all over the Roman Empire, there were
stone or timber forts built for permanent
units of the army. Inside the fort, the
soldiers lived in barrack blocks. These
were long buildings divided into at least ten
pairs of rooms. In one room were the bunks
for eight men and a fireplace for cooking
their meals. The other room was for their
equipment and weapons.

This is the Pont du Gard aqueduct, which carried water across the Gardon River to Nîmes, in southern France. The water ran in a channel at the top above arches nearly 1,650 ft (50 m) high. Each day it provided 420 qt (400 l) of water for each of the 50,000 people living in Nîmes. The aqueduct was over 30 mi (50 km) long.

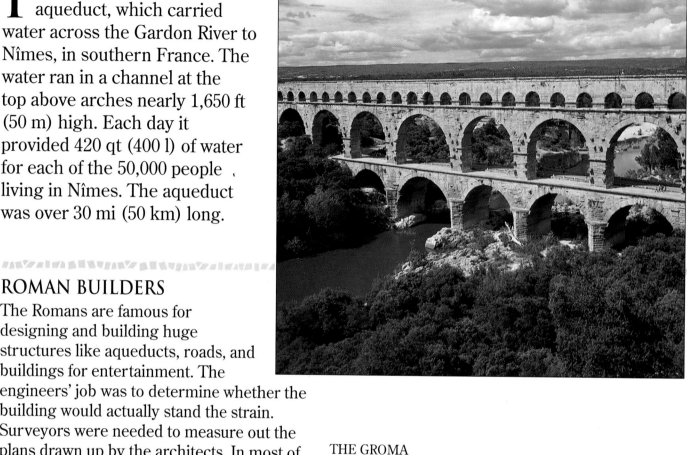

ROMAN BUILDERS

The Romans are famous for designing and building huge structures like aqueducts, roads, and buildings for entertainment. The engineers' job was to determine whether the building would actually stand the strain. Surveyors were needed to measure out the plans drawn up by the architects. In most of the countries they conquered, the Romans were the first people to build in brick and in stone held together by mortar (lime and sand mixed with water).

This is a surveyor's instrument, called a *groma*. It was used to mark out straight lines and was especially useful for engineers building straight roads.

THE GROMA

The surveyor would look over one of the arms of the *groma* and sight a straight line to someone holding a rod. Another person further away could then have his rod positioned on that straight line.

A Roman crane in action lifting blocks of stone for the aqueduct.

BUILDING THE AQUEDUCT

The Pont du Gard was built during the reign of the Emperor Augustus (27 B.C. to A.D. 14). The Roman engineers had a variety of "machinery" to help them build. Here you can see the great wooden device used for lifting blocks of stone. It is "powered" by people working the treadmill. Skilled workers cut the stone to the right shape for flat blocks or for the arches. At each stage of the aqueduct, the builders had to get the stones level using an instrument called a *chorobates*.

Many streets had fountains and water troughs filled by water piped through underground lead pipes. From here people could fetch the water they needed to use in their houses and "apartments."

R oman tombstones were often very elaborate and can tell us a lot about Roman life. This one was found in York, an important town in Roman Britain. Julia Velva (the person who has died) is shown on a couch at her own funeral feast surrounded by her family. The Romans believed that the gods controlled everything they did in life and the afterlife. They believed that after death, people went to the Underworld, a place they called Hades.

WORSHIP AT HOME AND IN THE TEMPLE

The Romans built special temples for their gods in which their statues were set up. They held processions and made sacrifices conducted by special priests.

Private altars were set up in houses and in some shops. Offerings would be made by the father on behalf of the family to the special "gods of the household."

Household altar

THE GODS

For most of the period of the Roman Empire, Roman people believed in a large number of gods. They even took on gods worshiped by other peoples, such as the Greeks and the Egyptians. Some Romans continued to worship Jesus Christ after he had been crucified, even though it was against the law. Christianity did in fact become the official religion of the Empire some years later.

MINERVA was the goddess of wisdom, crafts, trades, and industry. The Romans believed she invented musical instruments. She is often shown in armor because she guided fighters in battle.

Professional actors and musicians were employed to lead the funeral procession to the grave.

FUNERALS

At different times in the Roman period, people were either cremated (their bodies burned and the ashes collected in an urn) or buried. Cemeteries were only allowed outside the town walls and were usually at the sides of the road.

The Romans believed that the dead person would go on a journey to live with the gods of the dead, called the Manes.

JUPITER was the god of the sky and king of all the gods. He was called "the greatest and the best." His wife, Juno, was the patron goddess of women.

APOLLO was a Greek god worshiped by the Romans. He could tell the future and the Romans made offerings to him to reveal his secrets.

MITHRAS was originally worshiped by the Persians. Soldiers and merchants began to worship him and temples were put up all over the Empire where mysterious rites were carried out.

NEPTUNE was the god of water and the sea. He is usually shown with his three-pronged spear, called a trident.

ANSWERS TO MYSTERY OBJECT BOXES

Page 8: This piece of farm equipment was the equivalent of a modern combine harvester. It was called a *vallus*. Its wide blades were pushed by a donkey or an ox into the wheat crop. They cut off the heads and gathered them in a scoop.

Page 17: This little object is a personal toilet set, including an ear-scoop and a nail-cleaner.